U.S. ECONOMY IN THE MID-1800S

HISTORICAL TIMELINES FOR KIDS

AMERICAN HISTORIAN GUIDE FOR CHILDREN 5TH GRADE SOCIAL STUDIES

Speedy Publishing LLC

40 E. Main St. #1156

Newark, DE 19711

www.speedypublishing.com

Copyright 2017

In this book, we're going to talk about the United States Economy in the mid-1800s. So, let's get right to it!

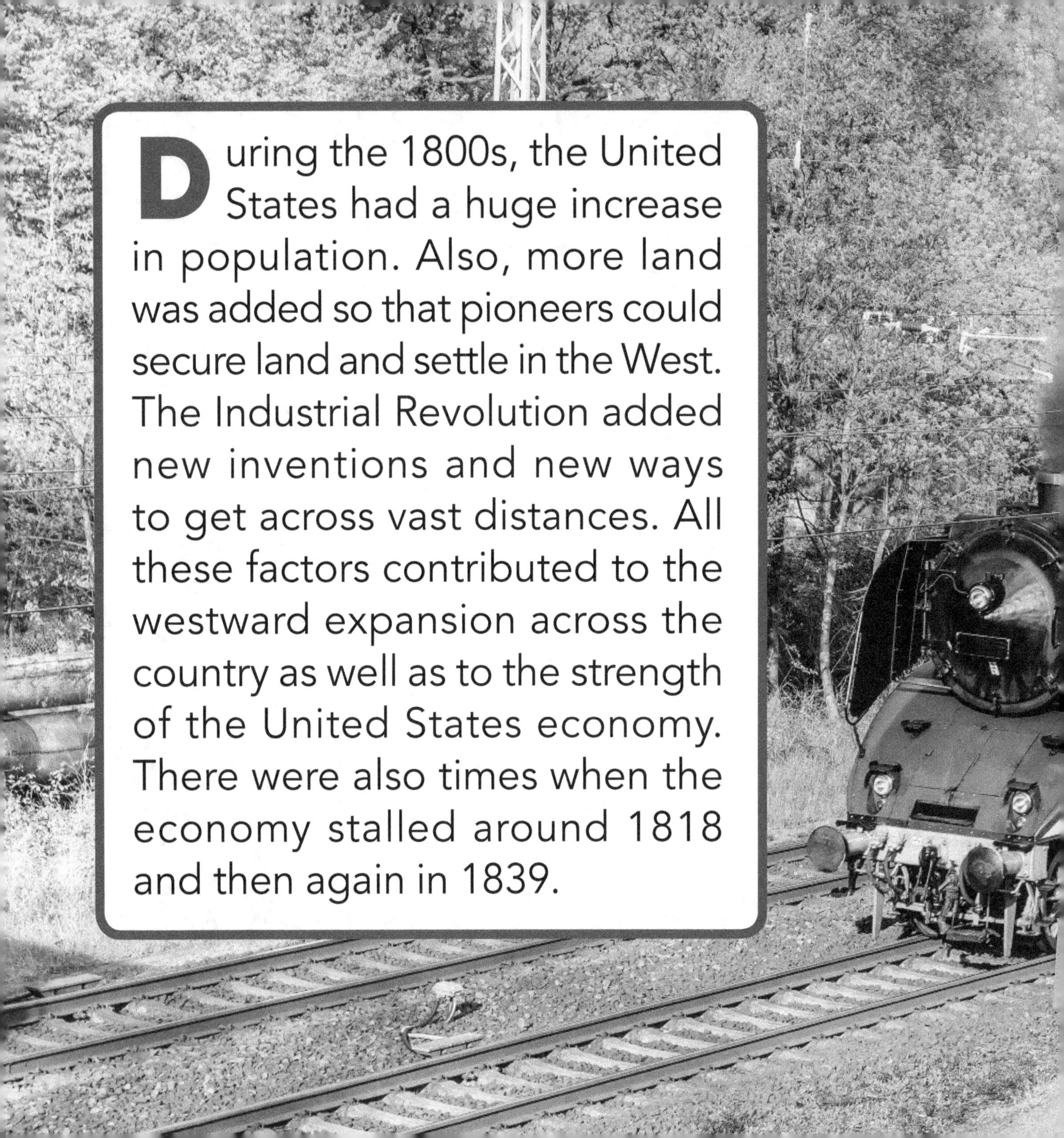

During the 1800s, the United States had a huge increase in population. Also, more land was added so that pioneers could secure land and settle in the West. The Industrial Revolution added new inventions and new ways to get across vast distances. All these factors contributed to the westward expansion across the country as well as to the strength of the United States economy. There were also times when the economy stalled around 1818 and then again in 1839.

THE POPULATION GROWS (1800–1850)

America had a second census in the year 1800. At the time, the population in the United States was around 5.3 million. However, by the time of the seventh census, which took place in 1850, the

population was over four times that amount, over 23.2 million. This increase was an enormous surge in population in a relatively short time.

The growth in the population was part of the reason that in the 1800s, people began to move out West, despite the dangers in doing so. At this point in time the West was truly the Wild West. The land was largely wilderness and very treacherous to cross. Some Native Americans were hostile toward the white settlers and there were always the natural dangers of raging rivers, searingly hot deserts, and poisonous snakes.

Despite these challenges, between the year 1820 and the year 1850, over four million people set out for lands in the West. Farmers needed more land to plant crops and raise livestock. This land wasn't available anymore on the crowded east coast. The economy was growing in huge spurts but there were also times of panic. These times, mainly in the year 1818 and then again in the year 1839, caused people to move west with the idea of starting all over to make a new life.

THE GOVERNMENT OPENS UP LAND (1803–1848)

President Thomas Jefferson saw the future of America when he purchased the Louisiana Territory from the French in 1803 for a mere $15 million. The Louisiana Purchase added over 530 million acres to the land in the United States, which more than doubled its landmass. The expedition by Lewis and Clark, from the year 1804 through 1806, led to amazing discoveries.

THOMAS JEFFERSON

The lands to the west were not only filled with natural beauty but they were also filled with resources for farmers, miners, and merchants.

The state of Florida and the section of the Gulf Coast that was located east of the Mississippi River was negotiated from Spain in 1819 in the Adams-Otis treaty.

United States settlers began to takeover land in Texas in the 1830s. Texas had already become independent from Mexico in 1836, which was ten years prior to the Mexican-American war. However, the Texans had slaves so the northern states didn't want them to come into the Union. When President James K. Polk was elected in 1844, he quickly pushed to get Texas as part of the United States.

GOLDEN FIELD, WILLAMETTE VALLEY, OREGON

A similar situation occurred in Oregon's Willamette Valley in the 1830s. American settlers started farms there on the fertile lands although it was not yet a part of the United States. In 1846, the United States negotiated with their former government Great Britain to establish the borders of the Oregon Territory, which became the northwestern states of Oregon and Washington as they are today.

The Mexican-American War took place from 1846 through 1848. President James K. Polk felt that the United States had what was termed a "manifest destiny." In other words, the United States was destined to be a great and powerful nation.

He and many others felt that in the future the United States would spread from "sea to shining sea."

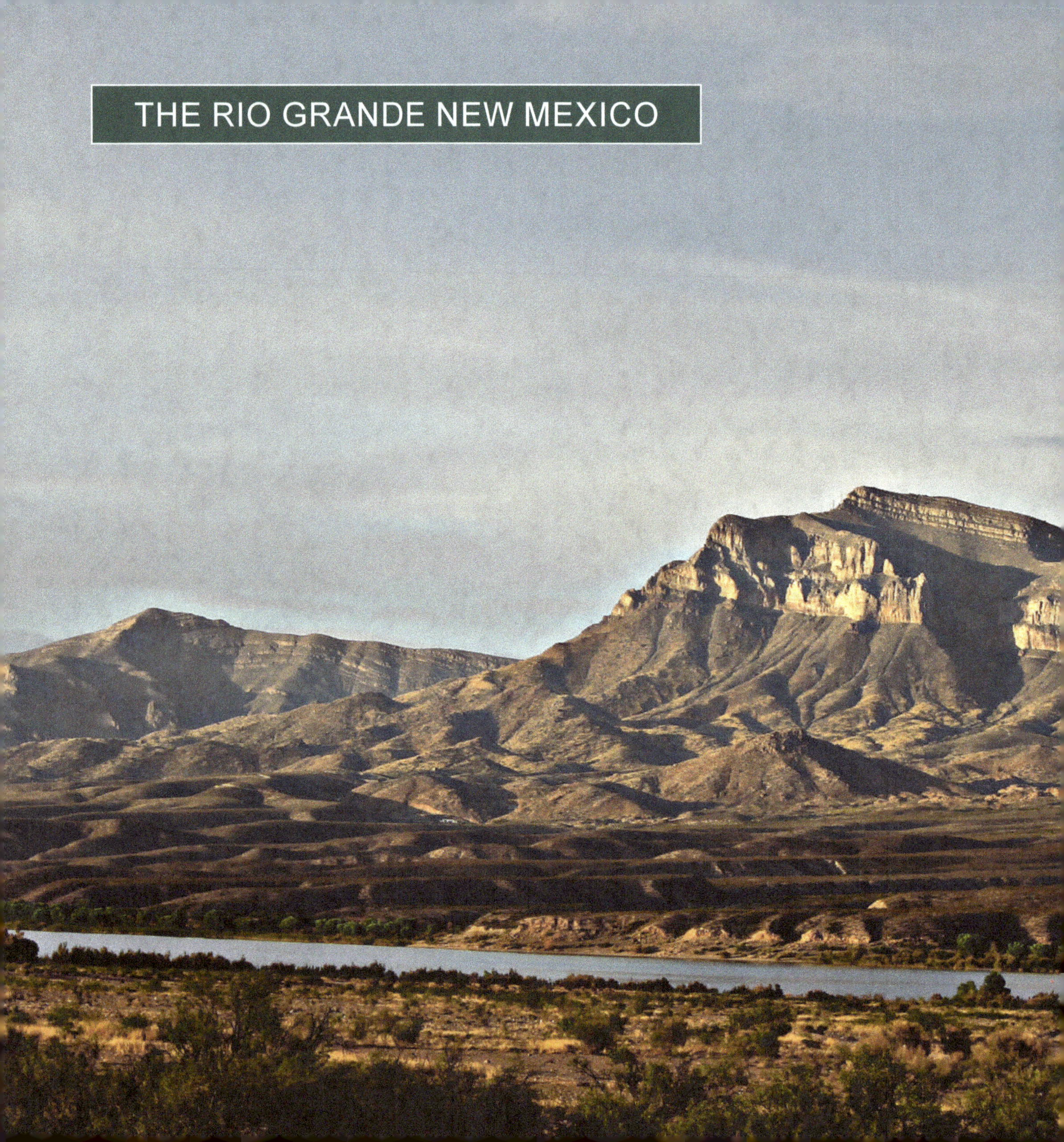

THE RIO GRANDE NEW MEXICO

A battle between the US and Mexico broke out along the Rio Grande river. The United States had one victory after another and when the war was over, the US had taken over one-third of the landmass that had formerly belonged to Mexico. The victory added land that would eventually become these Western States:

- Utah
- Nevada
- Arizona
- New Mexico
- California
- Portions of Wyoming and Colorado

The Mexican-American War increased US land by 25%.

Further negotiations with New Granada in Central America gave the United States rights over the Isthmus of Panama. There had been ongoing discussions about building a canal there to cut down

the time from shipping between the Atlantic and Pacific Oceans. The United States would build the Panama Canal in the next century.

GOLD STONE

THE GOLD RUSH (1848–1855)

Gold was found in California a few days before the land was handed over by the Mexican government to the United States. As soon as settlers heard the word "gold," they started to head out to California in huge numbers.

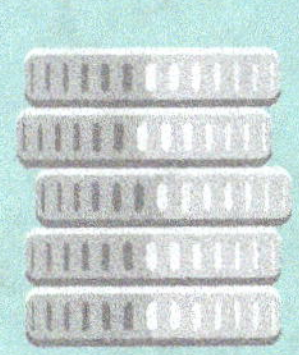

Over 300,000 people traveled across the country to try to "strike it rich." This event was called the "Gold Rush." It took place from 1848 when the gold was first discovered, until 1855.

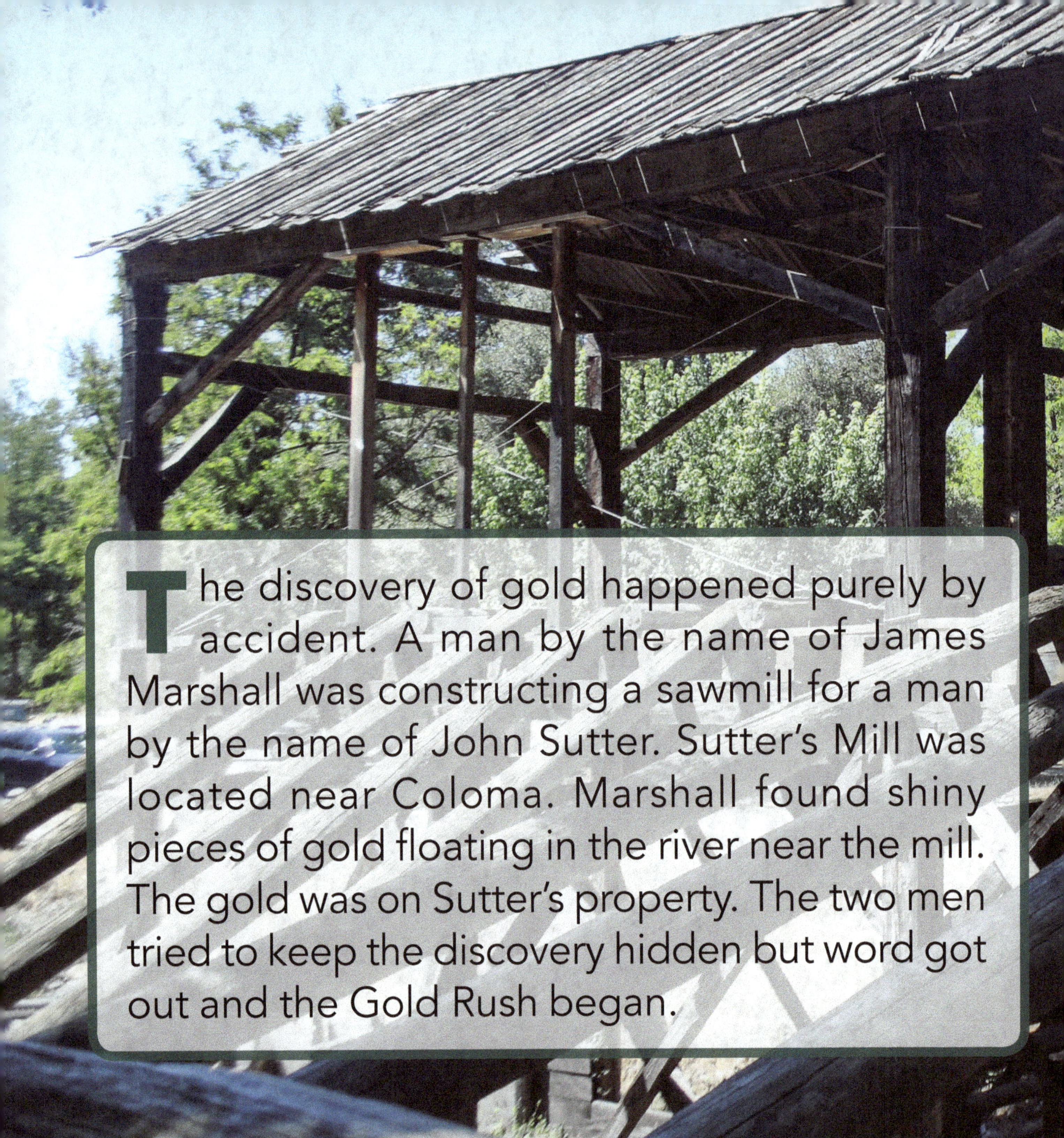

The discovery of gold happened purely by accident. A man by the name of James Marshall was constructing a sawmill for a man by the name of John Sutter. Sutter's Mill was located near Coloma. Marshall found shiny pieces of gold floating in the river near the mill. The gold was on Sutter's property. The two men tried to keep the discovery hidden but word got out and the Gold Rush began.

SUTTER'S MILL

Prior to the Gold Rush only about 14,000 settlers who were not Native Americans lived in California. By 1848, an additional 6,000 settlers had arrived and a year later about 90,000 people came to hunt for riches.

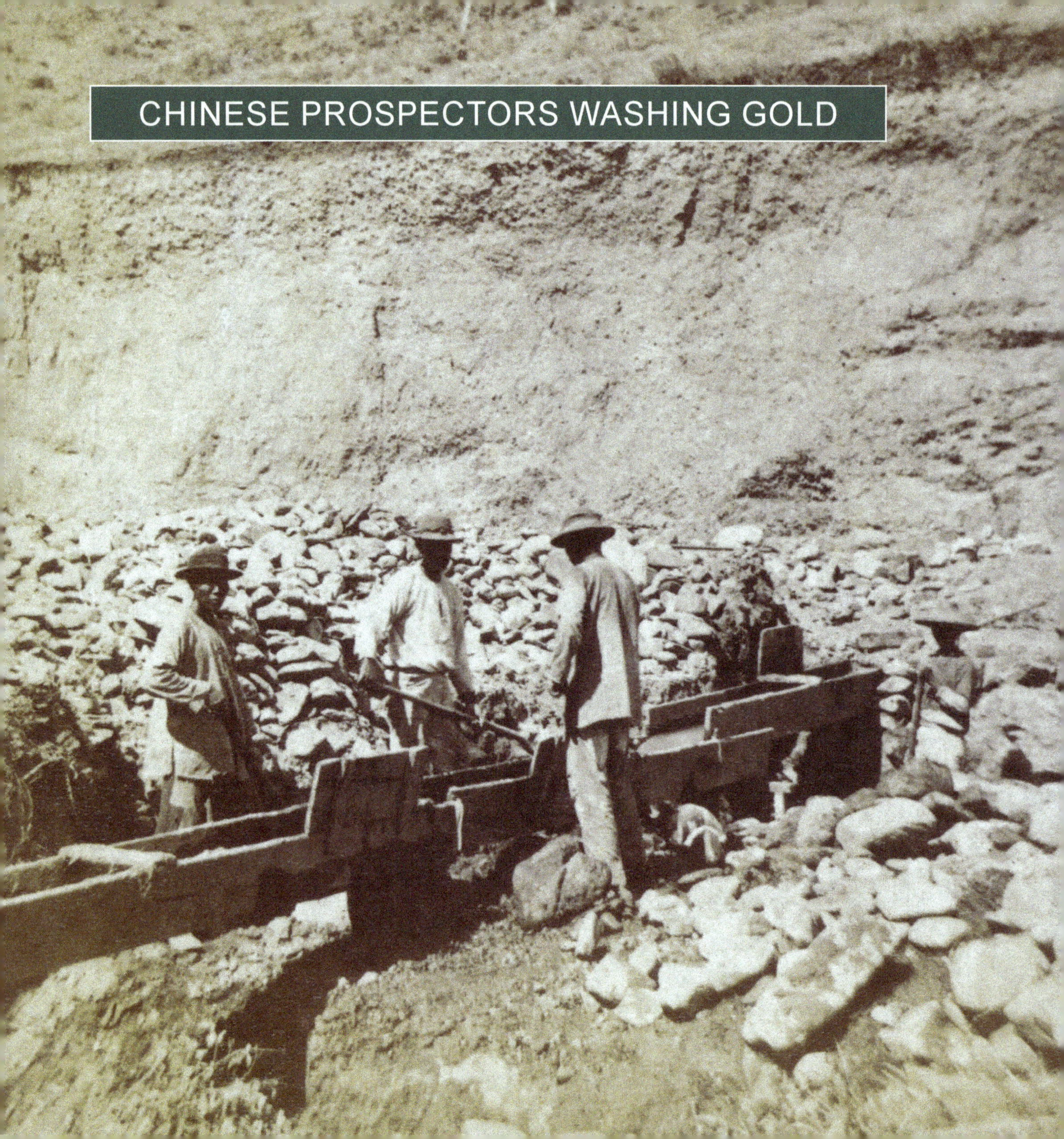

CHINESE PROSPECTORS WASHING GOLD

They were nicknamed the "Forty-niners" since they arrived in 1849. Most of the people who arrived to search for gold were from the United States, but there were also people from Europe, Australia, and China.

California became the 31st state during the Gold Rush. San Francisco, which had had only about 1,000 people, swelled to a population of 30,000. It's estimated that about 12,000,000 ounces of gold were found during the Gold Rush. In today's value

it would be about $16 billion worth. The land and gold in California were huge draws but there was something else valuable there as well, the Pacific Coast.

As the population of the United States expanded from the east coast to the west coast, there was a desire to open up seaports for trade. In 1844, the United States signed an agreement with China to open up importing and exporting between the two countries.

Industrial Growth in the United States (1820–1870)

During these decades of land expansion, there was also a revolution happening in industry. The Industrial Revolution had begun in Europe in the late 1700s and early 1800s. It soon spread to the northeast section of the US where fabric mills were the first to employ new machines and new labor forces to create mass-production textiles.

INTERIOR OF TEXTILE MILL

ABRAHAM LINCOLN

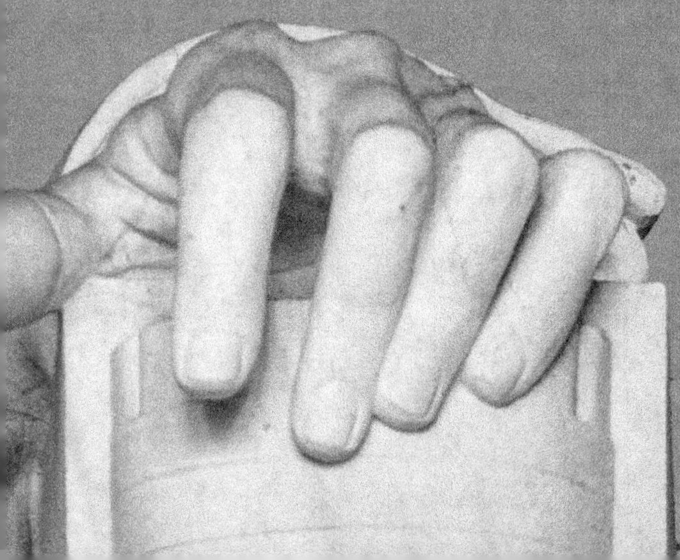

By the year 1860, when Lincoln came into office, over 15% of the United States population lived in cities and about one third of the economy was based on manufacturing instead of farming. Many immigrants from Europe saw the opportunity for a better life in the United States.

Between the years 1845 and 1855, over 300,000 Europeans came to the shores of the United States, every year. Many of them were poor when

they arrived on shore, but were quickly put to work in factories making cotton cloth, clothes from wool, shoes, or machinery.

The southern states were dependent on the North for capital as well as manufactured products. Their economy depended on slavery, which was protected as long as the South remained in power within the

federal government. However, in 1856, the North organized a new political party, the Republicans. Their interests represented the industries of the north.

In 1860, the Republicans supported Abraham Lincoln for President. He spoke about the abolishment of slavery, which, of course, made him unpopular in the slave-dependent southern states. However, several measures were pushed that helped the United States move to a more industrialized economy.

In 1861, a tariff was introduced to make US products more appealing to consumers than goods imported from Europe and Asia. This helped fuel growth of United States industries.

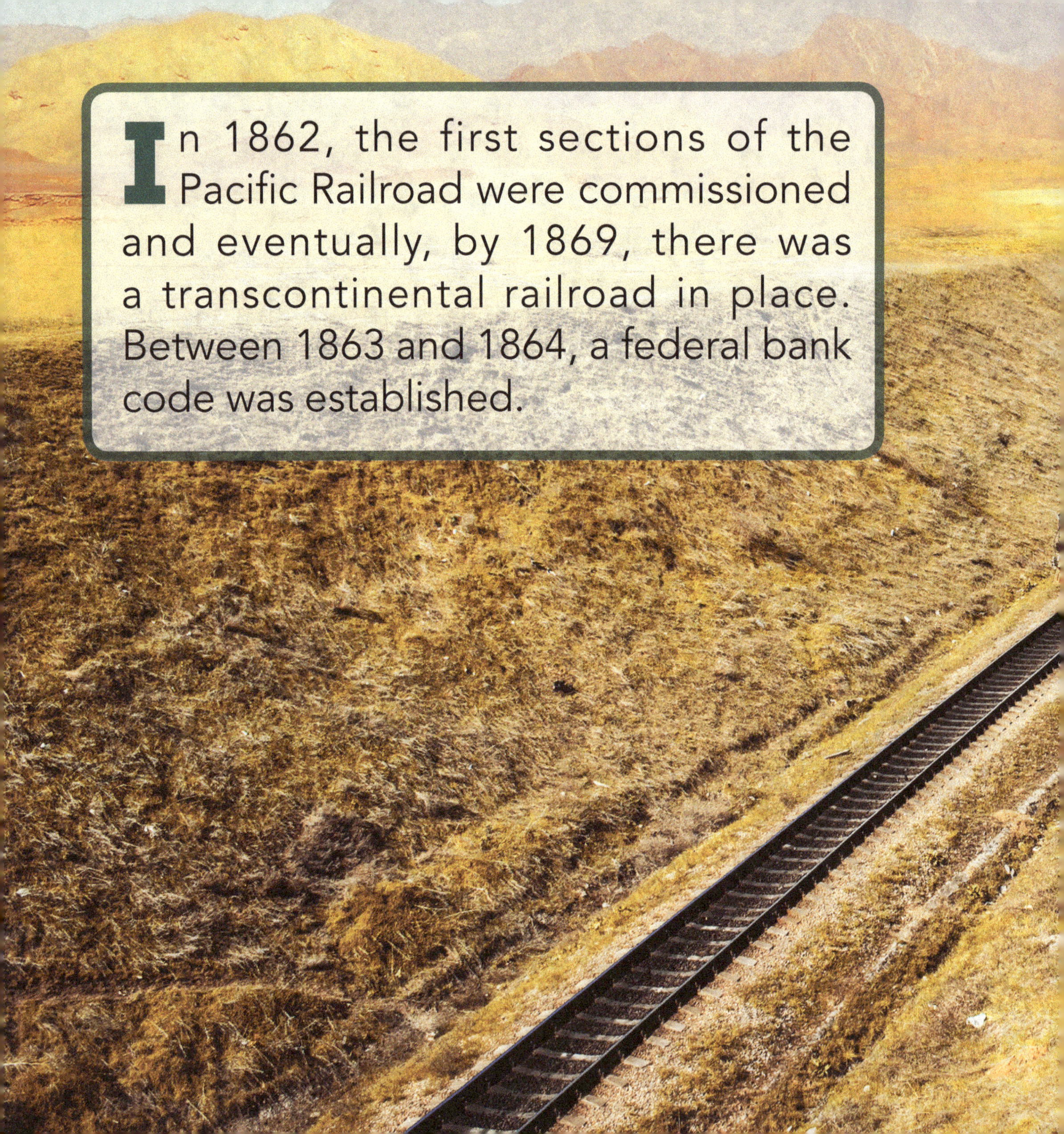
In 1862, the first sections of the Pacific Railroad were commissioned and eventually, by 1869, there was a transcontinental railroad in place. Between 1863 and 1864, a federal bank code was established.

After the North won the Civil War in 1865, the United States economy became based on northern industries, which had become even more profitable due to the war's demands.

The southern lifestyle, which had been based on slave labor, began to disappear and the northern industrialists became the dominant force in political and social life.

AFRICAN AMERICAN SLAVE FAMILY

WASHINGTON
OREGON
MONTANA
NORTH DAKOTA
MINNESOTA
IDAHO
SOUTH DAKOTA
WISCONSIN
MICHIGAN
MAINE
VERMONT
NEW HAMPSHIRE
NEW YORK
MASSACHUSETTS
CONNECTICUT
WYOMING
NEBRASKA
IOWA
NEVADA
CALIFORNIA
UTAH
COLORADO
KANSAS
MISSOURI
ILLINOIS
INDIANA
OHIO
PENNSYLVANIA
NEW JERSEY
WEST VIRGINIA
DC
MARYLAND
DELAWARE
KENTUCKY
VIRGINIA
ARIZONA
NEW MEXICO
OKLAHOMA
ARKANSAS
TENNESSEE
NORTH CAROLINA
SOUTH CAROLINA
TEXAS
LOUISIANA
MISSISSIPPI
ALABAMA
GEORGIA
FLORIDA
ALASKA

SUMMARY

During the 1800s, the United States had a huge increase in population. There was a push for "manifest destiny" as land was added and settlers began to populate the newly acquired lands in the West. At the same time, immigrants were coming to the northeast to work in the new industrial factories. The economy of the United States was strengthened through these land acquisitions, the Industrial Revolution, and the Gold Rush.

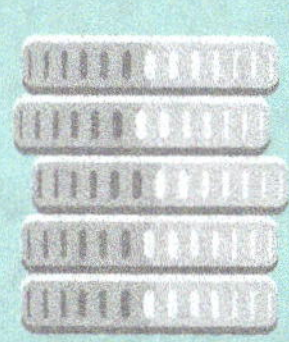
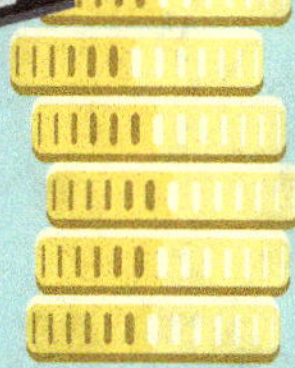

Awesome! Now that you've read about the United States Economy in the mid-1800s, you may want to read more about the Industrial Revolution in the *Baby Professor book Legacies of the Industrial Revolution: Steam Engine and Transportation – History Book for Kids.*

Visit

BABY PROFESSOR
EDUCATION KIDS

www.BabyProfessorBooks.com

to download Free Baby Professor eBooks
and view our catalog of new and exciting
Children's Books